crafting*on*the*go

ribbon

crafting*on*the*go

ribbon

sixth&spring
books

sixth&spring
books

233 Spring Street
New York, NY 10013

Copyright© 2004 by Sixth&Spring Books
All rights reserved including the right of reproduction in whole or in part in any form.

Library of Congress Cataloging-in-Publication Data

Crafting on the go!: Ribbon.
   p. cm.
ISBN 1-931543-53-4
1. Ribbon work I. Crafting on the go!

TT850.5.C73 2004
746'.0476--dc22   2003067326

Manufactured in China

13579108642

First Edition

contents

introduction

Ribbons have always had a way of making even the simplest things special. Our ancestors elaborately embellished clothing, accessories and home décor with ribbons. Some of us can remember our mothers ironing and tying our pretty hair ribbons. Winding and twirling pastel ribbons around a Maypole to signify the arrival of spring is another memorable tradition. There was something magical about seeing all the colors hanging together.

Ribbons can signify important events, from opening ceremonies to the celebration of maiden voyages. Winners are awarded blue ribbons to let everyone know who is the best. Ribbons are hung to announce someone's arrival home, to celebrate a special day or to show support for causes close to our hearts.

Wrapping, twisting, curling, folding, tying, stitching, weaving, embellishing—it all can be done with ribbon and the results make us happy! The myriad textures and colors excite our senses. Working creatively with ribbon is fun and easy and sparks our imagination. Even "mistakes" can be turned into design opportunities!

The projects presented in this book are designed to unleash your creative energy, and to inspire and encourage you on a journey into the world of ribbon.

ribbon glossary

There are so many choices! The most difficult part of working with ribbons is figuring out which type to use from the vast selection available. The following is a list of some types of ribbon, most of which were used to create the projects in this book.

A. Single and Double-Face Satin

Available in a large variety of widths and colors. Single-face satin has one shiny and one matte side. Double-face satin is shiny on both sides. Use double-face satin on projects where both sides of the ribbon will be seen.

B. Grosgrain

Available in a range of widths and colors. Grosgrain is tightly woven and has tiny vertical ridges. It is the same on both sides so it is suitable for many different kinds of projects.

C. Novelty

Includes all types of designs such as checks and plaids, ginghams, prints and metallics. Novelty ribbons are available in all textures, widths, wire-edge and not wired.

D. Picot-Edge

Ribbon with a looped edge, available in satins and sheers with satins.

E. Wire-Edge

RIbbon with a very narrow wire sewn into the edges. Easy to work with because the wire enables the ribbon to hold its shape. Works well for making bows, flowers, leaves and gathers. Available in many colors and widths.

F. Sheers and Sheers with Satins

Transparent, often with iridescent or metallic threads woven in. Often combined with satin. These ribbons have a very soft, elegant look.

G. Pre-Made Ribbon Flowers

Ribbon flowers are usually roses, but come in other styles as well. Very useful when a lot of roses are necessary. Available in a wide range of colors and "by-the-yard."

H. Silk Embroidery Ribbon

Used for ribbon embroidery. Available in a variety of colors and widths and usually made of 100% silk, polyester and rayon are available too. Silk is soft and smooth, and flows and curves nicely. Wonderful for home furnishings and fashion—the wider ribbons are even being used for knit and crochet!

I. Taffeta

An elegant, crisp fabric ribbon that is easy to work with. Iridescent and moiré styles are common. Adds a touch of elegance wherever it is used, from wrapping a special package to embellishing apparel.

J. Silk Fabric Ribbon

Elegant and soft ribbons in various widths and colors. Works well as an accent on elegant wearables or home-decorating projects.

K. Velvet

Lush ribbons in a variety of widths and colors. Available in synthetic or cotton. Beautiful in home decorating or fashion designs.

Ribbon Snippets

- Always cut ribbon with good dressmaker's scissors. Designate a pair that cuts only fabric and keep them sharp. Cut wire on wire-edged ribbon with wire cutters.

- Use a liquid sealer like Fray Check by Dritz™ to keep ribbon ends from raveling.

- Fusible webbing is great for adhering ribbon to many surfaces. When fusing, always use a pressing cloth to protect iron and ribbon from glue.

- Fabric glues like Beacon™ Fabri-Tac™ or Dritz™ Liquid Stitch are great for attaching ribbons to fabric. Glue sticks and double-sided tape also work well for a light hold.

- Press ribbons using a pressing cloth and a warm iron. Many synthetics will melt if the iron is too hot. Test iron on a scrap piece of ribbon first.

- Store ribbons on spools or tubes to help keep them crease-free.

- Most fabric ribbons can be carefully washed or dry cleaned. Check ribbon labels for cleaning instructions. Treat your ribbons as you would treat your clothes.

- Ribbons can be purchased at most fabric and craft stores. Look on-line as well (see the Resource Guide). Pay attention to the types of ribbon you are choosing. If you are making projects you want to last a long time, choose ribbons that are woven-edged, silk, rayon, organza, etc., rather than paper or plastic craft ribbons, which are not durable and don't have the same hand of better ribbons.

Embroidery Stitch Glossary

back stitch

spider web rose

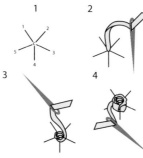

fly stitch

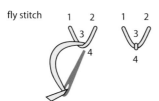

5

japanese ribbon stitch

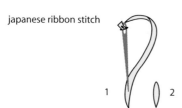

detached lazy daisy

colonial knot

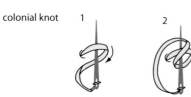

mark your place

Length of ⅜"(9mm)-wide woven-edge, double-face satin ribbon in desired color
Note: Both beaded ends of the bookmark should hang over the edges of the book. Cut ribbon approx. 1½"(3.8cm) longer than spine of the book you want to fit.

Beads as desired
The beads should graduate in size and vary in shape.

Sewing needle and matching thread

Beacon™ Fabri-Tac™ glue

Scissors

A beautiful bookmark makes a wonderful gift for a special book or journal. With some ribbon and a few beads, it's deceptively easy to craft.

1 Fold one ribbon end and tack with a few stitches. String the first bead onto ribbon, pulling end of ribbon partway through. String remaining beads onto ribbon.

2 Skip the last bead and run ribbon through second to last bead and up through the remaining beads. Knot ribbon as close to bead as possible.

3 Place a small amount of glue inside first bead. Carefully tuck a bit of the ribbon into the bead to secure.

4 Repeat as above on other end of ribbon.

la vie en rose

materials

- **One shadow box**

- **1yd (1m) of satin ribbon roses in desired color**

- **Approx. 110 ribbon roses in assorted colors with green leaves**

- **One piece of fabric cut to fit back inside panel of shadow box**

- **18"(45.7cm) of ³⁄₁₆"(5mm)-wide sheer ribbon in desired color**

- **One 3"(7.6cm) pressed-Styrofoam® wreath form**

- **Metal letter to spell "roses"** (available in the scrapbooking section of craft stores)

- **Sequin pins**

- **Six white, flat-head tacks**

- **Craft glue**

- **Double-stick tape** (optional)

- **Scissors**

Shadow boxes are neat little places to "make a scene" and display photos and other treasured objects. For the person who loves roses, this shadow box is the perfect addition to the bedroom, powder room or even the living room.

1 Remove glass from shadow box. Cover back inside panel with fabric, attaching edges with double-stick tape or craft glue.

2 Insert sequin pin through center of ribbon rose. Place a tiny amount of craft glue on pin tip then push pin into wreath form. Overlap roses slightly with leaves peeking out. Completely cover front and sides of wreath with roses.

3 Pin length of sheer ribbon to top of wreath for hanger.

4 Tie small "shoe-tie" bow from narrow sheer ribbon. Pin bow at wreath top, over hanger.

5 Using flat-head tack, secure top of ribbon hanger to top inside panel of box. Wreath should hang freely in the middle of the shadow box.

6 Cut two long (almost to bottom of box), two medium and one short length of roses by-the-yard.

7 Glue metal letters spelling out "roses" in between roses on ribbon. Tack ribbons evenly to top inside panel of box. Ribbons should hang just slightly in front of wreath, as shown in photo.

stripe it rich

Fresh flowers in a beautiful vase are a celebration in and of themselves! They can change a mood, a room or an ordinary day into a special one. Colors change with the seasons, so why not make the containers extra-special too—with ribbon!

materials

Any container with straight sides

Ribbons in assorted widths, colors and textures

Craft glue

Scissors

1 When choosing ribbons, establish a color scheme. It is helpful to find one ribbon you want to "feature" and build the look around it. Layering ribbons creates interest and adds texture.

2 Inexpensive glass or plastic vases work well, but don't limit yourself to the obvious. Cover a box in the same manner, then place any container that holds water inside. Stripe votive holders, fill with flowers and place them at each table setting.

3 Use dots of glue to adhere ribbons to the container, overlapping the ends at the back for a neat finish. Keep checking to make sure the stripes are straight!

4 Fill with coordinating flowers and celebrate!

napkin lariats
and place cards

materials

for one lariat

- 16"(40.6cm) of 1"(25mm)-wide grosgrain ribbon in desired color

- Decorative button or beads

- Sewing needle

- Gold or silver metallic thread

- Scissors

for one place card

- One round disk label (available at office supply stores or in the scrap-booking section of craft stores)

- One colored-paper tag with punched hole

- One press-on initial

- 7"(17.8cm) of ¼"(7mm)-wide ribbon in desired color

- Gold pen

This simple new twist on the napkin ring will dress up your table instantly. Also a great gift idea to add to beautiful napkins for the hostess. We used grosgrain ribbon, but any type of ribbon would work beautifully, depending on the occasion.

To create lariat

1 Make a 1"(2.5cm) loop in one ribbon end. Make two stitches and stitch button or beads on opposite side of ribbon.

2 Wrap lariat around napkin. Feed other ribbon end through loop and twist ribbon in side loop to secure.

Variation

Use two ribbon colors. Join two ribbons together where they go through the loop.

To create place cards

1 Rub initial onto disk. Write name on tag.

2 Fold length of ribbon in half. Feed folded end through back side of tag and disk. Loop loose ends of ribbon through folded loop (this is a lark's knot).

3 Decorate edges of tag with gold pen.

4 Tuck place card under lariat.

picture perfect

Embellishing a plain, wood frame with ribbons dresses up your favorite photos. These pretty framing ideas will inspire you to explore the possibilities. Basic craft skills and a little imagination are all it takes to turn the ordinary into the extraordinary.

materials

Unfinished-wood picture frame with 1 to 1½"-wide (2.54cm to 3.8cm) flat border

Assorted ribbons

Scissors

Beacon™ Fabri-Tac™ glue

1 Consider the photograph you intend to place in the frame. There may be colors or a theme that you would like to carry over into the ribbon design. Choose ribbons that will lay nicely and fit the frame's dimensions. Unwired ribbon will work better in most cases. Also decide how ribbons can be layered or woven. Once you have chosen the ribbons, the rest is easy! Consider incorporating other elements that add interest, such as beads, tassels or pre-made ribbon flowers.

2 Set the frame glass and backing aside. Remember that the glass, photo and backing need to fit back together, so keep the back side smooth if you need to fold and attach ribbons. The outside back of the frame also needs to be covered. Think about taking the design around to the back or cut a piece of black felt to fit and cover any unfinished ribbons.

3 Glue ribbons in place on frame, making sure there aren't any gaps. Glue carefully to avoid seepage through ribbons or on edges.

lighten up

Any lampshade with straight sides lends itself to ribbon striping. This is a great way to dress up an old lamp or personalize a new one. And, it makes coordinating your décor easy. Cover the whole shade with wild, bold stripes of ribbon or just use ribbon as an accent as we have done here.

materials

At least three ribbons in varying widths
Length will be determined by shade dimensions.

Beacon™ Fabri-Tac™ glue

Scissors

1 Remove shade from lamp. Determine desired layout of ribbons on shade.

2 Measure circumference of shade and cut ribbons 1"(2.5cm) longer than this measurement.

3 Using a small amount of glue, adhere ribbons to shade, making sure they are straight and smooth. If part of a ribbon isn't glued down, it will ripple and light will come through the opening.

4 To finish the seam at the back of the shade, fold ribbon ends under and glue to secure.

materials

- 1½yd (1.5m) each:
  - 3¾"(95mm)-wide iridescent green taffeta ribbon
  - 2"(50mm)-wide purple/gold woven rayon ribbon
  - 1¼"(30mm)-wide sheer iridescent purple ribbon
- 6" to 18"(15.2cm to 45.7cm) each of 2"(50mm)-wide sheer iridescent ribbon in purple, aqua, red and lavender
- Red seed beads
- 3mm flat beads
- 4mm and 5mm round beads or pearls
- Gold metallic sewing thread
- Beading needle and thread
- Sewing needle
- Scissors
- White glue

that's a wrap

This all-ribbon scarf, accented with a row of iridescent, ruffled flowers, is an easy way to add feminine flair to an outfit. The flowers are simple pinwheels made with sheer ribbon. They become even lovelier with shimmering beaded centers.

1 With gold thread, hand-stitch green taffeta, purple/gold rayon and sheer purple ribbons together, with sheer ribbon in the center.

2 Double-fold and hem both ends of scarf.

Make one 4"(10cm) large, one 2¾"(7cm) medium, five 1¾"(4.5cm) medium/small, and one 1¼"(3.3cm) small flower as follows:

3 For large and medium flowers, sew running stitches lengthwise along one ribbon edge. Pull thread to gather and knot in center. Overlap ends and stitch them together.

4 For medium/small and small flowers, fold ribbon in half lengthwise and run a gathering stitch through both edges. Pull thread and knot in center. Overlap ends and stitch.

5 Add beads in center of each flower as follows: Bring knotted thread through flower from back to front. String round bead then seed bead. Go back through round bead to back of scarf. String 3mm flat bead and seed bead at back. Go back through flat bead, skipping seed bead, take a small stitch and knot as close to beads as possible. Dab glue on knots to secure. Repeat to attach beads to remaining flower centers.

scarf back ⟶ | ⟵ scarf front

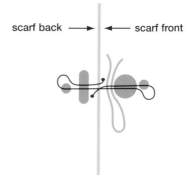

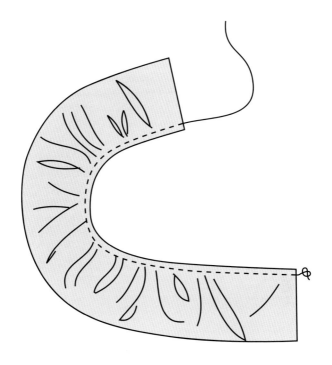

materials

Jersey-knit fabric in metallic gold

1½"(39mm)-wide wire-edge taffeta ribbon in iridescent gold

⅞"(23mm)-wide red velvet ribbon

Gold embroidered scroll appliqué

2"(50mm)-wide red sheer ribbon

Gold mini tassels

Pillow form or polyester fiberfill

Disappearing-ink fabric marker

Sewing needle and matching thread

Sewing machine

Straight pins

Fabric or craft glue
(optional)

ruffled romance

Beautiful decorator pillows can instantly refresh the look of any room with a little creative effort. Change your pillows every season, or at whim for a mini-makeover.

Note

To determine ruffled ribbon yardage—A 1"(2.5cm) ruffle requires approximately 2"(5cm) of ribbon. Determine pillow size, multiply measurement by two, multiply that by number of rows of ruffles. Allow approximately ½"(1.3cm) for seams. All other yardage is based on pillow size plus seam allowances.

1 Cut two panels from gold fabric to desired pillow size, adding ½"(1.3cm) for seams. On pillow front, measure and mark side seam allowances. Determine pillow center and mark.

2 Place sheer red ribbon on center of pillow front and pin in place. Ribbon ends should be approximately ½"(1.3cm) longer on each end. Center red velvet ribbon on top of sheer ribbon in the same manner; pin and set aside.

3 Cut wire-edge ribbon for each row. Tie a knot at one end of the first ribbon. Carefully poke wire from one of the ribbon seams at other end and gently gather ribbon on wire. As wire pulls out, keep your hand on the wire close to ribbon. Do not pull too hard. After each ruffle is made, knot and clip excess wire.

4 Pin ruffles in place on pillow on each side of red ribbons, leaving extra 1"(2.5cm) on each end for seam allowances. Space ruffles approximately ¼"(.7cm) apart. Hand-stitch ruffles in place.

5 Place front and back pillow pieces right sides together; sew seams, leaving an opening for turning. While stitching over ribbons, adjust them so they are laying properly. Turn pillow right side out.

6 Stitch or glue appliqué on top of center ribbon. Hand-stitch tassels in corners. Insert pillow form or fiberfill. Hand-stitch opening closed. Fluff ruffles.

materials

- 12"(30.5cm) square of taffeta fabric in desired color
- 12"(30.5cm) of 2"(50mm)-wide fancy Europa ribbon in desired color
- 1yd (1m) of ⅞"(23mm)-wide satin ribbon in desired color
- 12"(30.5cm) square of Heat n' Bond fusible web
- 1½yds (1.5m) of narrow satin cord decorative trim
- 10"(25.5cm) of ⅜"(10cm)-wide satin ribbon
- One 16mm glass bead
- One 4mm, 5mm and 6mm bead
- One 2"(5cm) beading head pin
- One 4"(10cm) and three 3"(7.6cm) circles of lightweight non-corrugated cardboard
- Handful of polyester fiberfill
- Beacon™ Fabri-Tac™ glue
- Scissors
- Needlenose pliers
- Iron
- Ruler

Victorian ladies wore chatelaines around their necks while sewing to keep pincushion and scissors on hand. This be-ribboned version is not only convenient, but charming as well! It looks beautiful hanging on a pretty hook in your sewing room or makes a lovely gift for your favorite seamstress.

Note

Ribbon will not be wide enough to cover cardboard circle. Piece ribbon to make it wide enough by placing one width of ribbon in center of circle. Cut the right and left sides off of a second piece of ribbon. Join edges to main ribbon, edge to edge, raw edges facing outside and glue. Cover where edges come together with decorative cord on top of seam (see diagrams).

1 Place fusible face down on wrong side of taffeta square and fuse with iron, following package directions.

2 Using 4"(10cm) cardboard circle (see template) as a pattern, cut three circles from taffeta. Cut ribbon strips to fit circle as in diagram and as noted above.

3 For scissors holder, iron a taffeta circle to one side of 4"(10cm) cardboard circle (see template). Turn circle over and iron on another taffeta circle. Mark where fold lines are indicated on this circle.

4 Place 4½"(11.4cm) length of 2"(50mm)-wide ribbon at an angle on one third of the circle, following fold line. Ribbon edge should overlap fold line approximately ½"(1.3cm). Glue ribbon to circle; trim ribbon along outside circle edge. Carefully glue decorative cording around edges of circle, twice. Cover where the ribbon was cut to fit at the fold; let dry.

5 Beginning with the smallest, string 3 beads onto head pin. With needlenose pliers, loop remaining head pin wire. Feed the ⅞"(23mm)-wide ribbon through the wire loop and glue. Place bead closest to the loop at the bottom edge of the circle. Glue ribbon flat in center of circle.

6 When glue is dry, place ruler at one fold line and carefully work cardboard into a fold, using the hard edge of ruler to keep it straight. Press firmly with fingers to get a smooth fold. Repeat on other fold line. Glue the two folded edges together, ribbon side on top.

7 For pincushion, iron remaining taffeta circle to center of one 3"(7.6cm) cardboard circle. Clip fabric edge at ½"(1.3cm) intervals. Fold edge over to wrong side and fuse in place. String 16mm bead onto other end of ⅞"(23mm)-wide ribbon, leaving a 3"(7.6cm) tail. Glue tail to uncovered side of cardboard circle, with bead coming out at top of circle; let dry. Knot ribbon above bead.

8 On another cardboard circle, place enough fiberfill stuffing to make a firm "pouf" for the pincushion. Carefully lay pieced ribbon from Step 2 on top of stuffing. Fold edge under and glue ribbon to cover cardboard.

9 Glue three cardboard circles together, making sure to center ribbon and bead at top.

10 Glue ⅜"(10mm) ribbon then three rows decorative trim around outside edge of pincushion.

template
cut 2
(one without fold lines)

1

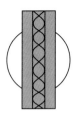

place one
ribbon in
center of
circle

2

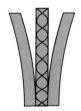

cut edges
from
second
ribbon

3

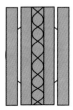

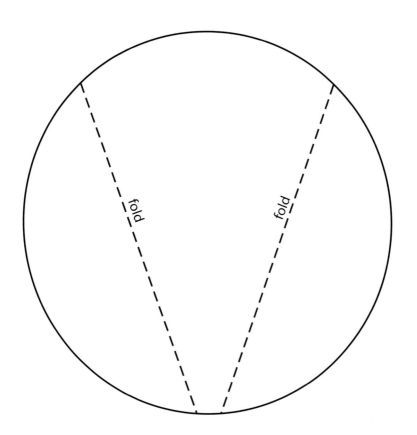

fold

fold

little rose bouquet

materials

1yd (1m) of 2¼"(56mm)-wide burgundy satin ribbon (makes one rose)

6"(15.3cm) of 2¼"(56mm)-wide hunter green satin ribbon (makes one leaf)

1yd (1m) of 2¼"(56mm) sheer ribbon in hunter green

Floral wire stems, 18 or 20-gauge, 12"(30.5cm) long

Green floral tape

Greening pins

Wire cutters

Sewing needle and threads to match burgundy and green ribbons

Container

Floral foam to fit in container

A small silver vase filled with beautiful, handmade satin roses looks elegant on a bedside table, powder-room shelf, or anywhere you want to add a touch of everlasting nature. Change the colors and the vase for a whole different look.

1 Before beginning flower, thread needle and knot thread.

Each flower is wrapped with a wire "stem" in the middle. Wrap wire stem in floral tape. Bend a loop at one end of wire.

2 Fold ribbon in half over wire loop and gather around stem with fingers. Roll ribbon into a cylinder to create flower center. Pinch bottom of ribbon and tack with two or three stitches to secure.

3 Fold ribbon down on right end so cylinder is horizontal and a 45° angle is created at the fold.

4 Holding ribbon with index finger, middle finger and thumb of one hand, fold and twist ribbon with other hand. Stitch through twist to hold. Turn flower, still holding with fingers and fold and twist ribbon for next layer; stitch layer; stitch (twisting and folding should be fairly loose). After flower is desired size, stitch and knot to secure. Still holding flower in one hand, begin to wrap bottom of flower with floral tape. Continue wrapping until excess ribbon is covered at bottom and taped to end of wire stem. Make several flowers in same manner to complete bouquet.

5 For leaf, lay ribbon horizontally. Fold left side down. Fold right side down to meet left side and make a point on top. Make a loop in taped wire, as with flowers, and insert loop into "v" of ribbon. Gather ribbon to wire stem at bottom, keeping wire enclosed in ribbon folds. Make a few stitches to secure gathers. Wrap ribbon and stem with floral tape same as for flower. Make a total of three or five leaves.

6 Insert floral foam into container and secure with craft glue.

7 To cover floral foam, ruffle sheer green ribbon around top edge of container and secure with greening pins.

8 Insert one rose in center of container, followed by side flowers. Fill in with remaining roses and leaves to create a round shape. Bend wire in flowers and leaves to create desired shape.

leaf

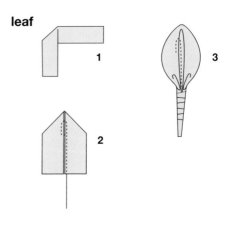

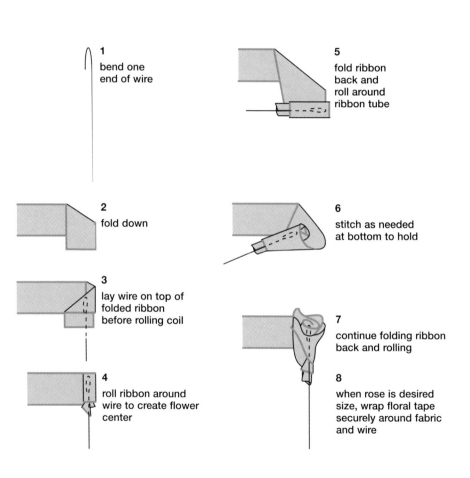

1
bend one
end of wire

2
fold down

3
lay wire on top of
folded ribbon
before rolling coil

4
roll ribbon around
wire to create flower
center

5
fold ribbon
back and
roll around
ribbon tube

6
stitch as needed
at bottom to hold

7
continue folding ribbon
back and rolling

8
when rose is desired
size, wrap floral tape
securely around fabric
and wire

materials

- **3yds (2.75m) of 1⅜"(34mm)-wide satin polka-dot ribbon** (for ruffle)
- **⅔yd (.6m) of 2"(50mm)-wide striped fabric ribbon** (for tie)
- **15"(38.2cm) of ⅞"(23mm)-wide brown satin ribbon** (for handle)
- **15"(38.2cm) of ⅝"(15mm)-wide dark brown satin ribbon** (for handle)
- **One 20" x 26"(50.8cm x 65cm) sheet of gray art paper** (if creating bags from scratch)
  Note: Both bags will fit on one sheet.
- **6"(15.3cm) square of light gray paper**
- **6"(15.3cm) square of decorative lacy-look paper**
- **Small decorative button or bead**
- **Double-sided tape**
- **Hole punch**
- **Craft glue**
- **Sewing needle and matching thread**
- **Scissors**

his-and-her totes

The perfect solution to gift-wrapping nightmares, this matching couple will be the hit of the party! It's great for toting gifts to the sophisticated host and hostess, or as bride and groom shower gifts. Make the entire bag yourself or take the decorating idea and apply to ready-made bags.

1 If creating bags from scratch, enlarge patterns (pages 46-47), trace onto art paper and cut out. Fold as marked. Glue in place with craft glue or double-sided tape.

2 Ribbon ruffle: Sew running stitches through length of ribbon in a zigzag pattern to create a series of triangles. At end, gently pull thread. Ribbon will gather in a flat ruffle. Knot thread when ruffle is the right size.

3 For bag flap, cut semicircle from decorative paper. Glue or tape in place on front of bag. Glue ruffle around edge of decorative paper. Add button or bead for clasp. Punch a hole on each side of bag. Knot one end of ⅞"(23mm)-wide ribbon and thread through punched hole from inside bag. Thread other end into opposite hole from outside bag; knot.

4 To make man's tie: cut one end of ribbon straight across. Glue each corner under to create a point. Tie other end into a loose knot. From lighter paper, cut shirt collar and glue to top of bag. Glue knot of tie on top of collar. Feed brown ribbon through top of bag as in Step 3.

her gift bag

stitch ribbon

gift bag templates
enlarge to measurements

shirt collar template
cut 2 (one for each side)

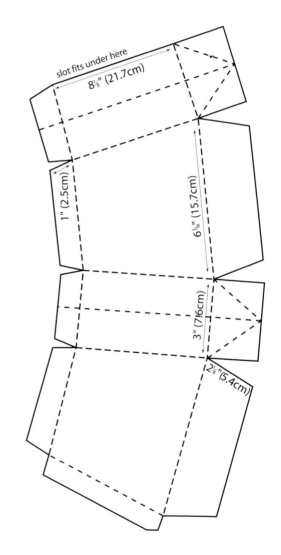

slot fits under here

8⅛" (21.7cm)

1" (2.5cm)

6³⁄₁₆" (15.7cm)

3" (7.6cm)

2⅛" (5.4cm)

his gift bag

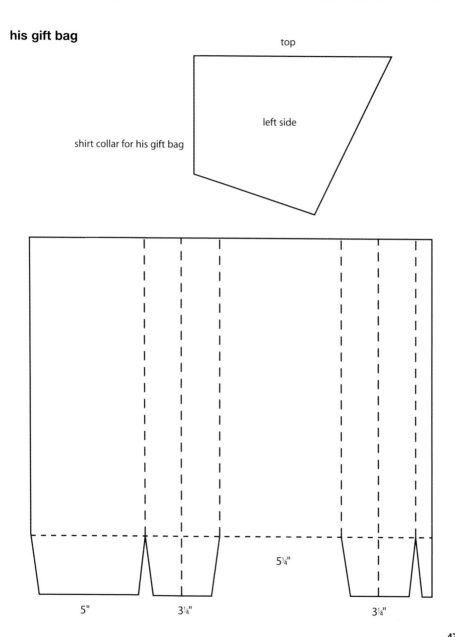

top

left side

shirt collar for his gift bag

5¼"

5"

3¼"

3¼"

heart to heart

Unfinished-wood hearts

Ribbon remnants in assorted colors, widths and styles

22-gauge craft wire in desired color

Assorted E-beads and seed beads

Metal words available in the scrapbooking section of craft stores

Acrylic craft paint in desired colors

Sponge brush

Sticky-back magnets

Clear-drying craft glue

Scissors

A be-ribboned twist on the refrigerator magnet! A great way to use up ribbon scraps and entertain the kids on a rainy day. Simply choose your favorite ribbons and glue them on painted-wood shapes.

1 Paint hearts with two to three coats acrylic, letting each coat dry before applying the next.

2 Cut assorted lengths of ribbon and crisscross on hearts as desired. Use ribbons longer than the shape so the ends hang off edges. When all ribbons are glued in place, cut around shape to trim.Layer different widths and outline hearts with narrow black ribbon if desired.

3 After all ribbon is in place, cut around shape to trim away excess. Wrap, loop and coil wire randomly around shape on top of ribbon design. String a few beads onto wire as you create loops and coils.

4 Glue words to shape where desired. Adhere magnets in place on back.

materials

- **1yd (1m) fleece**

- **5yds (4.5m) of 1½"(39mm)-wide ribbon**
  Purchase ribbon without wire edges or pull wires out before weaving.

- **Mini buttons or decorative trim** (optional)

- **Tailor's chalk**

- **Scissors**

- **Rotary cutter and cutting mat**

- **Metal-edged ruler**

- **Sewing needle and matching thread**
  Note: This blanket is for decoration or for holding baby only. Infants and small children should not be left alone with fleece, ribbon and trims. Fleece and most trims are not flame retardant.

nursery throw

A soft and cuddly fleece blanket, enhanced with a ribbon trim, is the perfect accent for the nursery. When mom rocks her baby to sleep, it's a wonderful occasion for them to snuggle up!

1 Lay fleece on cutting mat and cut off selvage edges.

2 Line fleece up with rule lines on mat. Slits for ribbon should be 1½"(3.9cm) apart and 1½"(3.9cm) wide. Begin cut lines 1½"(3.9cm) from edge. Mark cut lines with chalk or pen.

3 With scissors, cut each line.

4 Beginning in one corner, weave ribbon in and out of each slit. Ribbon should come up from the bottom of the blanket at each corner. Tie a knot at each corner when all ribbons are woven.

5 If desired, embellish with mini buttons.

materials

- **Cigar box or papier mâché or unfinished-wood container**

- **1½yds (1.5m) of 2"(5cm)-wide iridescent ribbon each in purple/copper and blue/grey**

- **2yds (2m) of ⅛"(3mm)-wide each metallic gold grosgrain ribbon and dark green metallic fabric ribbon**

- **1yd (1m) of 1½"(39mm)-wide metallic sage green fabric ribbon**

- **1yd (1m) of 2"(5cm)-wide sheer red ribbon**

- **Acrylic craft paint in antique gold**

- **Gold spray paint**

- **Satin-finish acrylic spray varnish**

- **Sponge stencil brush**

- **Small leaf rubber stamp**

- **Scrap paper**

- **Beacon™ Fabri-Tac™ glue**

- **Scissors**

mr. postman

Jazz up a cigar box with decorative ribbons to create a personalized stationery box. For matching stationery, use the same ribbons to embellish cards and envelopes.

1 Cover work surface and protect surrounding area with newspaper to prevent overspray. Following label directions, apply two coats paint to inside and outside of box. Let each coat dry before applying the next. Spray box with varnish following manufacturer's instructions. Let dry.

2 Cut eight to nine squares and rectangles from 2"(5cm)-wide ribbon, four or five from each color.

3 Practice stamping on scrap paper first. Dab paint onto leaf stamp using stencil brush. Place ribbon on scrap paper to prevent paint from bleeding through. Stamp leaf design in alternating directions on both sides of ribbon. When dry, gently pull threads from both ends of ribbon to create fringe.

4 Arrange and adhere ribbons on box top as desired. Use small dots of glue only on ribbon edges.

5 Adhere edges of three ribbons vertically to inside box lid for storing stamps, envelopes, extra paper, etc. If desired, stamp leaf design on ribbons before attaching. Stamp a length of ribbon with the leaf design to tie around handmade cards. Trim box with other ribbons as desired.

6 For matching stationery, purchase plain cards and envelopes in a coordinating color. Stamp and fringe ribbon as above and use to decorate cards and envelopes. Tie cards with stamped ribbon.

- **Two 32"(81.2cm) lengths of 2"(5cm)-wide sheer ribbon in two colors**
- **16"(40.8cm) of 2"(5cm)-wide sheer ribbon in third color**
- **2"(5cm) square of plastic template material**
- **Wooden craft stick**
- **2½yds (2.3m) of ⅛"(3mm)-wide silk ribbon in desired color**
- **16 beads in graduating sizes and shapes; including two 3mm beads**
- **Sewing needle and matching thread**
- **Beacon™ Fabri-Tac™ glue**
- **Scissors**
- **Essential oil in desired fragrance**
- **Cotton ball**

scents-sational

A sweet fragrance offers a hint of romance to any environment. This dainty sachet is so simple to make, you'll love adding your favorite scent and hanging it in a special place.

1 With needle, punch tiny hole in center of plastic square.

2 Place glue on center of plastic square. Lay one 32"(81.2cm)-long ribbon across square at the ribbon center point.

3 Lay second 32"(81.2cm)-long ribbon across plastic square in opposite direction of first at the center point. Press ribbon into glue using wooden craft stick. Set aside to dry.

4 String beads on thread beginning with bead that will be stitched closest to the bottom of the plastic. String 5 beads of alternating sizes and colors, going from largest to smallest. Turn last bead on its side, feed string through it then feed string back through the first beads. Feed thread through hole at bottom of plastic.

5 Zigzag-fold 16"(40.8cm) ribbon on top of plastic piece, threading each fold onto needle. String last two beads onto needle and pull beads down on poufs of ribbon. Feed needle back through plastic ribbon pouf, then through the same hole and knot. Secure knots with glue.

6 Cut a 12"(30.4cm) length of ⅛"(3mm) silk ribbon. Fold sides of sachet up and gather together, leaving streamers at top. Wrap 1⁄16" ribbon around gathered area and knot. Thread remaining piece of silk ribbon into needle. Sew ribbon through gathered area twice, keeping ends even. Remove needle. Thread several beads, from largest to smallest, onto both strands of ribbon. Double-knot ribbon at top of last bead. (Remaining ribbon lengths are the hangers.)

7 Thread a couple of beads onto streamer ends of gathering ribbon.

8 Add dots of glue to all knots, beads and ribbon ends to prevent fraying.

9 Cover a cotton ball with fragrance and slip inside sachet or add fragrance to ribbon pouf inside sachet. Refresh as needed.

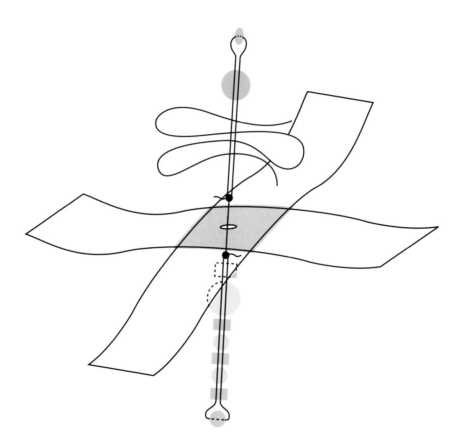

materials

girl's pocket

Three ¾" x 10"(19mm x 25.4cm) pieces of ribbon in different colors

Two ³⁄₁₆" x 10"(5mm x 25.4cm) lengths of pink and green satin ribbon

One ³⁄₁₆" x 8"(5mm x 20.3cm) piece of green satin ribbon (for handle)

Two pink ribbon roses

White embroidery floss and embroidery needle

boy's pocket

One 1" x 10"(25mm x 25.4cm) piece of ribbon

Two ¾" x 10"(19mm x 25.4cm) pieces of ribbon

One ³⁄₈" x 8"(9mm x 20.3cm) piece of ribbon (for handle)

One wooden button

Black embroidery floss and embroidery needle

Beacon™ Fabri-Tac™ glue

Scissors

tooth fairy pockets

This pint-sized pocket keeps your little one's tooth safe until the fairy comes. Featuring ribbon rose accents and a blanket-stitch edging, the pocket hangs safely on a bedpost, dresser knob or the wall just above the pillow.

Finished size (one pocket): approximately 2½"(6.3cm) square

1 Lay 10"(25.4cm) lengths of wider ribbon side by side on work surface. Glue edges of each ribbon together. Lay remaining ribbon(s) on top of seams and glue in place.

2 Fold ribbon piece in half and finger-press then open flat. Fold each end to the middle crease. Fold two ends together to create pocket.

3 Glue hanger in place at each corner of pocket.

4 With embroidery floss, blanket-stitch around sides and bottom of pocket.

5 Glue on embellishments.

materials

- **Ribbon in assorted widths, styles and colors**
- **8"(20.3cm) wire wreath frame**
- **½yd (.5m) of beaded fringe**
- **Glittery or faceted craft beads in pastel colors**
- **Crystal leaf-and-bead garland**
- **22-gauge floral wire**
- **Spray paint in silver or as desired**
- **Newspapers**
- **Beacon™ Fabri-Tac™ glue**
- **Scissors**
- **Wire cutters**

This elegant wind dancer is a great decoration to hang outside the bride's home, at a garden reception or above the dance floor—let your imagination run wild! All you need are lots of twirly ribbons, some pretty beads, a few little bells and a halo of fresh flowers.

1 Work in a well-ventilated area. Cover work surface and protect surrounding area with newspaper to prevent overspray. Following label directions, apply 2 coats paint to wire wreath, letting each coat dry before applying next.

2 Cut ribbon to desired lengths for hanging. [Ours ranges from 18"(45.7cm) to 32"(82.4cm).]

3 Place wreath on work surface, curved side facing up. For hangers, tie four ribbons, evenly spaced at the top. Hang wreath from a plant hanger, an over-the-door coat hanger or something similar. It will be easier to work with if the wreath is hanging.

4 Tie or loop and glue ribbon streamers to center of wreath, alternating ribbon colors, lengths and styles. (Note: Start with a few ribbons, adding more as needed.) Work around center of wreath then proceed outward. Keep in mind that the wind dancer needs to move in the breeze and is prettier if light shines through it. Use more sheer ribbon than satin. Very narrow ribbons will also flow nicely.

5 Add streamers of beads as desired, either by stringing beads on narrow ribbon and hanging or by looping pre-strung beads over wire frame and gluing.

6 When all streamers are attached, glue beaded fringe around outside edge of wreath frame. Trim ribbon ends as needed.

7 Using short lengths of floral wire, attach leaf-and-bead garland around top edge of wreath.

If adding fresh flowers to the "crown," proceed as follows:

1 Soak floral foam in water. With knife, cut foam into smaller pieces to fit into wreath frame. Place plastic wrap on top of wreath frame, and floral foam on top of plastic. This will create a water base in which to insert flowers.

2 Cut greenery and flower stems short. Insert greenery then flowers into foam. (Some suggested greenery and flowers are: ivy, asparagus fern, freesia, babies breath, tea roses, stephanotis, mini carnations, and mini orchids.)

vintage comfort

materials

- ½ yard (.5m) of dark lavender silk shantung fabric

- 5yds (4.75m) of 7mm silk ribbon in mauve

- 5yds (4.75m) each of 4mm silk ribbon in hunter green and taupe

- 4yds (4m) of 4mm variegated silk ribbon in green tones

- Sewing needle and thread to match pillow fabric

- #22 chenille needle

- Tracing paper

- Tailor's chalk

- 5"(127mm) embroidery hoop

- Pillow form or polyester fiberfill

Ribbon embroidery is a beautiful form of stitchery that was used by Victorian women to create intricate works of art. Now, ribbon embroidery is more popular than ever and can be used to accent bedspreads, towels, blankets, pillows and more! The stitches used are basic and a cinch to master.

Finished size: to fit an 8½" x 11"(21.6cm x 29.2cm) pillow

1 Cut one 15½" x 18½"(39.3cm x 47cm) piece and one 9½" x 12½"(24cm x 31.7cm) piece from shantung. Set aside smaller piece.

2 Sew a basting line 4"(10cm) from edge all around larger fabric piece.

3 To draw vine pattern on fabric, place pattern on a window or light box with fabric on top. Trace pattern onto fabric. (Test marker on a scrap piece of fabric to make sure it disappears with damp paper towel.) Working within basting lines, trace pattern in different places on fabric to create an all-over design.

4 Embroider vine branches in variegated green ribbon using backstitch (see page 13). As you bring needle up through fabric, be careful not to pierce ribbon already stitched. Use your finger to gently move ribbon to the side.

5 Use mauve ribbon to embroider detached lazy-daisy flowers. (Note: The base of the lazy-daisy flowers will be close to the vine, see page 13.)

6 Attach a bud to the vine using a fly stitch (see page 13) and hunter green ribbon.

7 Embroider leaves in Japanese ribbon stitch (see page 13) using hunter green. Remember to lay ribbon gently as you pierce the tip—pull ribbon through gently so leaves don't lose curl at the top.

8 Scatter flower buds made with taupe colonial knots.

9 Trim embroidered fabric piece to same size as small fabric piece. Sew pillow front and back together using ½" (1.3cm) seams and leaving a 6" (15.2cm) opening along center of bottom edge. Insert pillow form or fiberfill; slipstitch opening closed.

Another great idea

10 Accent a pillow with spider-web roses (see page 13). You'll need 7mm mauve and 4mm hunter green silk embroidery ribbon, a chenille needle, a sewing needle, matching thread and small beads.

11 Thread sewing needle with matching thread and create five spokes as in diagram. Stitch five spokes to radiate from the center. Form spoke stitches by coming up on the outside then going down into the center as in diagram. Knot end.

12 Thread embroidery needle with a 12" (30.5cm) length of mauve ribbon. Bring needle up through fabric as close as possible to center.

13 Weave ribbon over one spoke, then under the next. Proceed in this manner clockwise around the spoke until all spokes are covered. Do not pull ribbon too tightly as you go around the rose. Let the ribbons gently twist. As you stitch, adjust ribbons so not all turn toward center.

14 Add a pair of lazy-daisy leaves to rose using hunter green ribbon (see page 13). Make lazy daisy as close to rose as possible, almost underneath outer petals.

15 Attach small beads to rose center using sewing needle and thread.

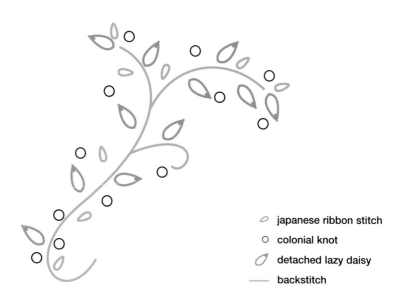

◦ **japanese ribbon stitch**

○ **colonial knot**

⟋ **detached lazy daisy**

—— **backstitch**

spring tote

materials

- ½yd (.5m) pale yellow satin brocade fabric
- 1½yds (1.5m) of ⅞"(23mm)-wide sheer rainbow ribbon
- 1½yds (1.5m) of ⅜"(9mm)-wide gold metallic ribbon
- 24"(60cm) of ⅜"(9mm)-wide gold metallic ribbon (for handle)
- Beacon™ Fabri-Tac™ glue
- Four butterfly appliqués
- Sewing needle and matching thread
- Sewing machine
- Fusible web (optional)
- Scissors

A girl can never have too many pretty evening bags, and this quick-make carry all is made extra special when accented with whimsical butterflies. Change colors and fabrics and the possibilities are endless.

1 Cut four 6½" x 7½"(16.4cm x 19cm) rectangles from fabric (two for lining and two for bag). If desired, choose a different fabric for lining.

2 Sew or fuse sheer ribbon to right side of bag front in horizontal rows.

3 Sew or fuse gold ribbon on top of sheer ribbon beginning at top of bag then skipping two ribbons, and continuing in this manner to bottom of bag.

4 Sew bag and lining as follows:

    a Cut two 12"(30cm) of gold metallic ribbon for handles. Pin one ribbon handle to top right side of bag back with loop laying on bag fabric (diagram A).

    b With right sides facing, sew front lining and bag front at top with handle sandwiched in between.

c Repeat with back lining and bag back with other handle sandwiched between (diagram B).

d Place bag front (with lining attached and spread out) and back pieces together, right sides facing. Stitch around all sides, leaving an opening on what would be the lining bottom seam (diagram C).

e To square off bottom of bag, spread fabric apart at bottom seam so seam is flat and centered. At each corner, sew a straight line as though making the bottom line of a triangle with the seam (diagram D).

f Turn bag right side out through opening in lining. Fold bottom seam of lining in and whipstitch closed. Arrange lining inside bag. If desired, turn bag inside out and tack lining bottom to inside of bag.

5 Adhere butterfly appliqués to bag front with fabric glue.

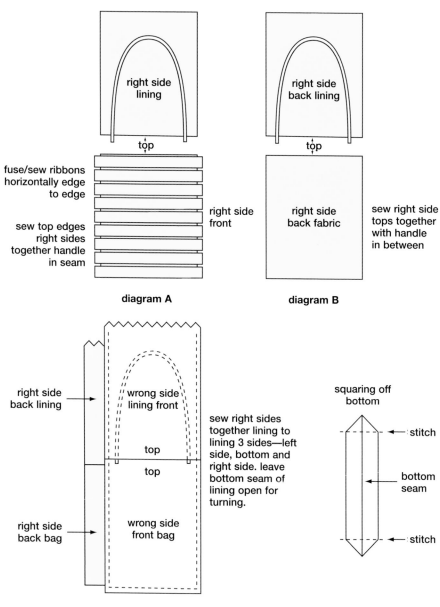

right side lining

top

right side back lining

top

fuse/sew ribbons horizontally edge to edge

sew top edges right sides together handle in seam

right side front

right side back fabric

sew right side tops together with handle in between

diagram A

diagram B

right side back lining

wrong side lining front

top

top

right side back bag

wrong side front bag

sew right sides together lining to lining 3 sides—left side, bottom and right side. leave bottom seam of lining open for turning.

squaring off bottom

stitch

bottom seam

stitch

diagram C

stitch sophistication

Though classic in design, this unique tank is thoroughly contemporary. By tying the ribbons together and pulling them through to the purl side, butterflies are created and this tank becomes reversible.

materials

Eight spools of 7/16"(10mm)-wide Hanah Silk Ribbons (by Artemis) in Tuscany

Size 11(8mm) circular needle or size needed to obtain gauge

Size G/6(4mm) crochet hook

Stitch holders

Scissors

Stitch marker

Finished size: 19" wide x 22" long (48.2cm x 55.8cm)

About silk ribbons

The ribbons come on 40yd (37m) bias-cut spools composed of 20 joined strips, each approximately 6'(1.8m) long. To prepare for knitting, all joins should be cut out of 7 of the 8 spools as they may come apart with dry cleaning or washing. To join ribbons, tie together with a square knot (right over left and under, left over right and under). You have just made a butterfly!

Finished bust: 38"(96.5cm)
Finished length: 22"(56cm)

Gauge: 3 stitches and 4 rows = 1"(2.5cm) over St st using size 11(8mm) needles. Take time to check gauge.

1 On circular needle, cast on 114 stitches. Place marker and join last stitch to first stitch, making sure stitches are not twisted.

2 Work in Stockinette stitch (knit every round) for 14"(35.5cm).

3 Place 57 stitches onto a stitch holder.

4 Work back and forth in Stockinette stitch (knit one row, purl one row). Bind off 4 stitches at the beginning of the next 2 rows, then 3 stitches, then 2 stitches—39 stitches.

5 When garment measures 17"(43cm), knit 16, join another spool of ribbon and bind off 7 center stitches, knit to end.

6 Working both sides at once, at the neck edge, bind off 3 stitches, then 2 stitches, then knit 2 stitches together twice (9 stitches).

7 Knit both straps until they measure 22"(56cm) from beginning; place straps on a holder.

8 Repeat Steps 4–7 on other 57 stitches.

9 Knit the front and back straps together.

10 Pull all butterflies to purl side of garment.

11 With crochet hook, single crochet around armholes and neckline, being careful to maintain measurements.

12 Tie additional butterflies around bottom of tank top as desired.

notable note hanger

A new twist on the bulletin board! Keep track of cherished mementoes or important events by slipping notes, letters or cards between beautiful ribbons fastened with eyelets.

materials

1yd (1m) of 3"(77mm)-wide tapestry ribbon

1yd (1m) of 2"(50mm)-wide sheer ribbon

12"(30.4cm) of ¼"(7mm)-wide coordinating ribbon (for hanger)

Two 5"(12.7cm)-long wooden dowels, ⅜"(9mm) in diameter

Four ⅜"(9mm) wooden finials

28 copper-colored 7mm eyelets and eyelet setter

Acrylic craft paint

Paint brush

Cutting mat with rule lines

Ruler

Tailor's chalk

Finished size: 32"(81.2cm) long

1 Paint two dowels and four finials with two to three coats acrylic, letting each coat dry before applying the next.

2 Lay tapestry ribbon flat on cutting mat. Center 2"(50mm)-wide sheer ribbon on top of tapestry ribbon.

3 Eyelets are punched through both ribbons to hold in place. Using ruler, place a mark on ribbon where eyelets should go. It takes four eyelets to form a "pocket" or slot in the ribbon. Some slots are larger than others. We made seven 3"(7.6cm) pockets, two 5"(12.7cm) pockets and one 4"(10cm) pocket. Eyelet is placed just in from ribbon edge.

4 Following manufacturer's instructions, apply eyelets where marked. If needed, pin top ribbon in place while punching eyelets.

5 Put dowels and finials together. Wrap top and bottom of tapestry ribbon around dowel rods and insert two more eyelets on each end to hold in place. (Opening should be smaller than dowel rod so it doesn't slip through.)

6 Tie ribbon hanger at top. If desired, add a few narrow ribbons and tie them into a bow leaving some long streamers on both sides of the hanger. Tie small beads onto streamers.

- **Small photo album**
- **Fabric** (to cover front and back of album cover and inside cover and back), **plus 3"(7.6cm) on all sides for folding**
- **2"(50mm)-wide organza ribbon in two styles**
- **½"(13mm)-wide organza ribbon**
- **Decorative cording in coordinating colors**
- **7mm ivory and 4mm taupe silk embroidery ribbon**
- **Antique glass seed beads**
- **#22 chenille needle**
- **Beading needle and matching thread**
- **Straight pins**
- **Sewing needle and matching thread**
- **Tailor's chalk**
- **Thin batting** (to cover front and back of photo album)
- **Double-sided tape**
- **Scissors**

wedding day memories

A treasured photo album becomes even more meaningful when the cover is lovingly handmade. Ribbon embroidery over sheer ribbons makes a delicate and beautiful album.

Note

Depending on album style, cover may be made from one piece of fabric and wrapped over the spine, or front and back will be made separately. Take this into consideration as you plan.

1 Lay out fabric for front cover on flat work surface.

2 Pin ribbons vertically to fabric, edges touching and alternating between 2"(50mm) and ½"(13mm) widths. Baste ribbons at top edge of fabric to hold in place. At bottom edge of fabric, weave 2"(50mm)-wide organza ribbon horizontally over and under the vertical ribbons. Baste in place at edges of fabric. (Ribbon embroidery and beading will hold ribbons in place.)

3 Decorate first 2"(50mm)-wide ribbon at left side of album cover with a heart as follows:

Pencil-trace heart shape onto ribbon. With beading needle and thread, outline heart design with glass beads. Knot thread at back. Referring to diagrams on page 13, embroider bow, lazy-daisy leaves, and colonial knot flower buds.

4 On center 2"(50mm) ribbon, embroider an ivory spider-web rose (see page 13). Add beads to center of rose. Embroider lazy-daisy leaves using taupe ribbon.

5 On third 2"(50mm) ribbon, stitch two ivory rosebuds. Stitch beads to center of each rosebud. Add taupe fly stitch and a Japanese ribbon-stitch leaf (see page 13).

6 On each narrow ribbon, stitch beads as desired. Stitch decorative cording horizontally over the tops of all ribbons.

7 Cut a piece of batting slightly smaller than front cover. Adhere to cover with double-sided tape.

8 Fold fabric edges under ¼"(.6cm) and hem. If needed, carefully press with cool iron. (Use a pressing cloth to avoid melting ribbon.) Center cover on album and fold top edge in at the corners. Fold right end in and pin to top edge. Fold bottom edge in and pin to top edge. (You are making a sleeve to slip over album. If you are working with a single piece of fabric for the whole album, continue the above for back cover. Carefully stitch corners together and slip on over batting.)

9 If desired, make a tie by stitching ribbons to edges of front and back covers. Tie ribbon in a bow.

materials

Ribbon is for one rose, 2½"(6.3cm) to 3"(7.6cm) across.

1½yds (1.5m) of 2"(50mm)-wide, double-faced, woven ribbon in rayon or polyester
Note: Ribbon should be soft and drape well. Roses are placed close together in rows from edge to edge on pillow top. Ribbon colors are alternated. Shown are lavender ribbons woven with silver metallic threads and purple ribbons woven with copper metallic threads.

Fabric as desired for pillow

Pillow form or polyester fiberfill

Sewing needle and matching thread

Straight pins

Sewing machine

Scissors

delightful rose pillow

This pillow is a sophisticated accent for a favorite room. Choose a monochromatic color scheme and see how it adds a touch of simple elegance to your décor.

1 Cut pillow fabric pieces to desired size. Pin front to back, right sides facing. Sew front and back together, leaving one side open for turning, attaching flowers and stuffing. Turn right side out and set aside.

2 For center of rose, roll one end of ribbon 3 or 4 times counterclockwise in a coil. Holding coil with thumb and index finger, use other hand to stitch through coil to hold in place.

3 Holding coil in one hand, fold ribbon away from you at a downward angle. Stitch petal to secure. Center coil should not be higher than "petals." Keeping bottom edge of ribbon fairly even with bottom of coil, continue to roll and fold ribbon back at an angle around coil, stitching as needed to hold in place. It may be more comfortable to move flower from hand to hand as you roll, pinch and stitch the flower.

4 As rose gets larger, begin to fold and twist ribbon loosely to achieve a fuller, more natural effect.

5 When rose is desired size, stitch ribbon end and knot thread. Repeat to make enough roses to cover pillow top. (Note: It is not necessary for each rose to be identical. Making them distinct adds interest and charm.)

6 Lay out and pin all roses to pillow top in desired arrangement. Carefully insert pillow form or polyfill to make sure roses are close enough together once the pillow is stuffed. Remove pillow form or polyfill. Stitch each rose to pillow top.

7 Insert pillow form or fiberfill into pillow and whipstitch opening closed.

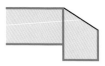

roll ribbon into tube

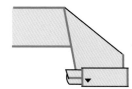

fold fabric back and roll around tube

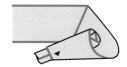

continue to fold ribbon back and roll. stitch as needed to hold in place

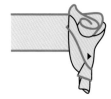

continue folding the rose from this point more casually

after rose is wrapped to desired size, fold bottom up and stitch

materials

One pair of purchased flip-flops

for each

25"(63.5cm) of 1½"(39mm)-wide ribbon in orange, yellow, and lime plaid

12"(30.4cm) of ⅞"(23mm)-wide ribbon in tangerine and yellow polka dot

12"(30.4cm) of ⅞"(23mm)-wide ribbon in yellow with pink edge

Six ⁷⁄₁₆" buttons

Small amount of polyester fiberfill

Bodkin or safety pin

Beacon™ Fabri-Tac™ glue

Sewing needle and matching thread

Scissors

tropical flip-flops

Show off beautifully manicured toes in these bright and sassy flip-flops. It's a quick change from a plastic strap to this be-ribboned pair. Choose your favorite colors to match your cover-up or tote and head for the beach.

1 With scissors, cut plastic straps off flip-flops.

2 Cut the 25"(63.5cm) piece of plaid ribbon in half. If ribbon is wire-edged, gently pull wire out from both sides of ribbon and discard.

3 Turn ribbon lengthwise, wrong side out. Whipstitch ribbon edges together to form a tube. Attach bodkin or safety pin to one end and push ribbon inside itself to turn tube right side out. Repeat to form a second tube from remaining length of plaid ribbon.

4 Fill each ribbon tube with small amount of fiberfill, leaving approximately 3"(7.6cm) on each end unfilled. Stuffing should make tubes slightly round.

5 Place approximately 2"(5cm) of glue on top of one ribbon end. Lay the other ribbon on top of glue and finger-press the two pieces together. Add more glue on bottom side of the piece just glued, and roll ribbon into a smaller tube. This piece will fit through the hole for the thong.

6 Pull rolled end of ribbon through hole from the top of the flip-flop to the sole. Pull ribbon through hole approximately 2"(5cm). Fold rough edge of ribbon end up approximately 1"(2.5cm) and sew button on top of folded end.

7 Place glue in the hole and around the indentation made from the original plug. Gently pull ribbon from top of flip-flop, bringing the button into the indentation. Press button firmly in place and pull ribbon for a tight fit in the hole. Add more glue if necessary. Straighten ribbon as needed so front side of ribbon roll is facing out and inside where toe rubs is smooth. If it appears to be rough, add more glue, fold and twist until ribbon is in the proper position.

8 Repeat as above for each strap. Try on flip-flops and measure to your foot to determine how long the straps should be. Pull ribbon ends through holes, making sure seams are facing in, and double check fit of straps. When satisfied with fit, cut away excess ribbon, allowing for the amount that goes through the hole. Repeat button attachments as in Step 7.

9 For flower, sew running stitches along one edge of polka-dot ribbon. At end, gently pull thread to gather ribbon, then knot and cut thread.

10 Re-thread needle and knot. Holding one end of ribbon with one hand, use other hand to twist it into a spiral, with gathered edge at bottom and ruffle at top. As needed, stitch at bottom edge to secure spiral. Knot thread when flower is approximately 2½" (6.3cm) across.

11 For leaves and flower center, cut yellow ribbon into four 3" (7.6cm) pieces. Loop three ribbons in half and stitch to bottom of flower. Loosely knot fourth piece and glue in center of flower.

12 Place flower on strap. Sew straps together where flower will be placed. Position flower and stitch to strap.

13 Repeat steps to complete second flip-flop.

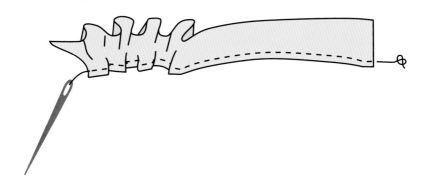

seaside sheers

This easy window treatment will brighten a dreary window and let the sun shine in. Warning: May stir up fond memories of long walks on the beach collecting seashells.

materials

- ¾"(9mm) and 1"(25mm)-wide sheer ribbons in light blue, light yellow, light green, and ivory

- Assorted shells

- Spring rod or other decorative curtain rod

- Beacon™ Fabri-Tac™ glue

- Scissors

- Newspapers

1 Measure window height and width. Determine desired ribbon length and double measurement. Depending on width of ribbons, determine how many ribbons you'll need to cover width of window. (Note: It is helpful to work on the rod at the window to determine length and layout of each ribbon.) Cover windowsill with newspaper to protect from dripping glue. Drape ribbons over rod.

3 Glue shells in place on the bottom of each ribbon.

Alternative method

Loop one end of ribbon and glue to create a rod pocket. Repeat on all ribbons. Vary ribbon lengths as above, hanging one shell on each ribbon.

looped-ribbon evening shawl

Looped ribbon fringes dresses up a soft and silky chiffon cover-up. The scarf offers maximum appeal for any formal ocassion.

materials

**2yds (2m) of 45"
(114.3cm)-wide chiffon
fabric**

**29yds (26.5m) of
⅜"(9mm)-wide Europa
iridescent ribbon**

**Sewing needle and
thread to match ribbon
and fabric colors**

Scissors

Sewing machine

Notes

Loops are created using one continuous piece of ribbon on each end of scarf. Each ribbon loop is 6"(15.2cm) long. There are approximately 86 loops at each end. If ribbon needs pressing, use a warm iron and a pressing cloth.

1 Hem both scarf ends by machine or by hand.

2 Beginning at one end of scarf, fold one ribbon end twice and stitch to scarf over hem. Fold first 3"(7.6cm) ribbon loop and tack to hemline. Stitch second ribbon loop to scarf, overlapping first loop at a 45° angle.

3 Repeat as above on other end of scarf.

4 Stitch selvage edges of scarf together, right sides facing; leave ends open. Turn scarf right side out and sew ends closed.

resources

Artemis, Inc.
179 High Street
South Portland, ME 04106
888-233-5187
www.artemisinc.com
(on-line catalog)

**Beacon Adhesives
Company, Inc.**
125 MacQuesten Parkway
South Mount Vernon, NY
10550
914-699-3400
http://beaconcreates.com

**Berwick-Offray Ribbon,
LLC.**
PO Box 601
Chester, NJ 07930
908-879-4700
www.offray.com

Blue Moon Beads
7855 Hayvenhurst Avenue
Van Nuys, CA 91406
800-377-6715
www.bluemoonbeads.com

Europa Imports Inc.
1528 Montague Expressway
San Jose, CA 95131
800-778-0717
www.europatrimmings.com

Mokuba New York
55 West 39th Street
New York, NY 10018
212-869-8900

ribbon

Editorial Director
Trisha Malcolm

Editor
Teri Daniels

Art Director
Chi Ling Moy

Designers
Teri Daniels
Jackie Ollom
Maria Tapia-Arana Rosa Designs
Hanah Exley
Tyler Tannhauser

Graphic Designer
Andrea Grieco

Technical Editor
Pat Harste

Copy Editor
Lisa Ventry

Illustrator
Ryan Brunetti

Photography
Jack Deutsch Studios

Project Manager
Michelle Lo

Production Manager
David Joinnides

President and Publisher, Sixth&Spring Books
Art Joinnides